P9-CCL-041

PROJECT SCIENCE

SKY AND WEATHER

Alan Ward

Franklin Watts

New York • Chicago • London • Toronto • Sydney

© 1992 Franklin Watts

Franklin Watts, Inc.
95 Madison Avenue
New York, NY 10016

Library of Congress Cataloging-in-Publication Data

Ward, Alan, 1932-
    Sky and weather / by Alan Ward.
        p. cm. — (Project science)
    Includes index.
    Summary: Uses simple projects and activities to introduce the sky,
stars, moon, and planets and the changes that can be observed in the
weather.
    ISBN 0-531-14176-4
    1. Weather—Juvenile literature.   2. Sky—Juvenile literature.
3. Astronomy—Juvenile literature.   [1. Weather—Experiments.
2. Astronomy—Experiments.   3. Experiments.]   I. Title.
II. Series: Ward, Alan, 1932-   Project science.
QC981.3.W37   1993   92-369
551.5—dc20   CIP AC

Series Editor : A. Patricia Sechi
Editor : Jane Walker
Design : Mike Snell
Illustrations : Alex Pang and Raymond Turvey
Typesetting : Spectrum, London

Printed in Great Britain

All rights reserved

CONTENTS

EARTH, MOON, AND SUN

The sun is, in fact, a rather small star. But it happens to be much closer to the earth than the other stars. Therefore the sun appears to be the biggest star in the sky. The moon is a lot smaller than the sun, but it seems to be about the same size. This is because the moon is nearly 400 times closer to the earth than the sun.

Danger!
Never look directly at the sun. Its dazzling brightness could damage your eyes or even blind you.

YOU NEED:
- 4 double sheets of large-size newspaper
- white glue or glue stick
- a push pin
- a yardstick
- about 4 feet of thread
- a pencil
- scissors
- blue and green felt-tipped pens

Comparing sizes

Glue together the edges of the sheets of newspaper to make one large sheet. Tie the thread in a loop that is about 2 feet long. Using a push pin and a pencil, draw a circle with a diameter of 3½ feet on the newspaper. Cut out the circle. This represents the sun.

Near the edge of this big circle, draw a circle with a diameter of 10 mm. Color it blue. This circle represents the earth.

Draw a second circle with a diameter of 0.1 inch. Color it green. This circle represents the moon. Tape the paper to a wall.

You will be amazed at this scale model, showing how the sizes of the earth, the moon, and the sun compare with each other.

Their actual sizes are:
Earth 7,926.4 miles in diameter
Moon 2,160 miles in diameter
Sun 535,680 miles in diameter

Day and night

We often imagine that the earth has an enormous rod that passes right through its North and South poles. This imaginary rod is called the earth's axis.

A model Earth

You can make a model of the earth and its axis by pushing the knitting needle through the center of the orange.

Hold the "axis" upright in front of the lamp or window — the bright light represents the sun. The half of the orange that faces the model sun is well lit, but the other half is much darker.

YOU NEED:

- an orange
- a knitting needle
- a lamp or sunlight streaming through a window

Be careful not to hurt anyone with the needle.

If your orange were the real world, it would be daytime on the lit side of the earth, and night time on the darker side.

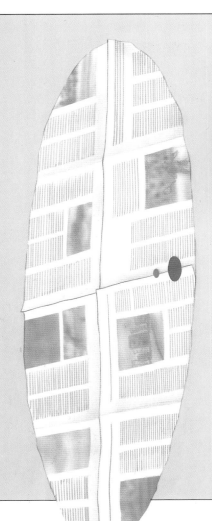

Did you know?

The earth rotates all the way around on its imaginary axis once every 23 hours, 56 minutes. Although it looks to us as if the sun rises, travels across the sky, and then sets, it is really the earth that is moving. People on the side of the world having night can see the distant stars. During the day these stars are invisible because the closest star, our sun, shines so brilliantly.

ECLIPSES OF THE SUN

The earth moves in a path through space called an orbit. The earth takes a year to travel around, or orbit, the sun. At the same time, the moon is traveling around the earth. The moon takes about a month to orbit the earth.

The sun casts long, cone-shaped shadows of the earth and moon. You might think these shadows look like witches' hats. The earth's shadow in space is about 620,000 miles long. The moon's shadow is long enough to reach the earth.

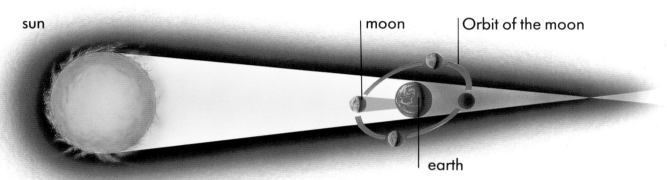

sun · moon · Orbit of the moon · earth

Eclipses

If you look carefully at the drawing above, you might think that the moon's shadow falls on the earth once a month. But this does not happen so often, because the orbit of the moon is slanted, compared with the orbit of the earth.

When the moon's shadow does fall on the earth, we say that there is an eclipse of the sun. If you are standing well inside the moon's shadow, the sun is blotted out by the moon. The world around you gets as dark as night for a few minutes. It is called a total eclipse of the sun. It is an exciting, mysterious experience.

If you happen to be near the edge of the moon's shadow, you can see how the moon covers only a bit of the sun. This is called a partial eclipse of the sun. You must take safety precautions if you want to watch such an eclipse.

You can see an eclipse of the moon when the full moon passes through the earth's shadow in space.

How to watch an eclipse

If you want to watch an eclipse, you must follow carefully the instructions below.

The newspapers will tell you when an eclipse is due to take place. You can watch an eclipse of the moon through binoculars. First, you will see a smoky haze, then a "bite" of deep shadow. If the eclipse is a total one, the white face of the moon will turn a reddish-brown color.

You must not use binoculars to watch an eclipse of the sun. It is dangerous to look directly at the sun. Instead, use this safe method of watching an eclipse of the sun.

YOU NEED:
- binoculars
- a square of black cardboard 24 inches × 24 inches
- a darning needle
- a sheet of white paper

Use the darning needle to make a hole in the center of the black cardboard.

Now hold the cardboard up to the sunlight so that the sun's rays can pass through the small hole.

Move the black cardboard until a round image of the sun is projected onto a sheet of white paper placed behind the cardboard. As the moon moves in front of the sun, a bite-like piece will disappear from the edge of the sun's image on the paper.

Did you know?

Although the diameter of the sun is about 400 times bigger than the diameter of the moon, the sun and the moon appear to be the same size. This is because the sun is 400 times farther away from the earth than is the moon.

You can prove this by taping the paper sun you made on page 4 to a wall 400 feet away. Push a ball of modeling clay, with a $\frac{1}{2}$-inch diameter, onto the end of a toothpick. Hold up the stick about 12 inches in front of your eyes. Now compare it with the paper sun. You will be able to eclipse the huge sun with your tiny model moon.

WHY DO WE HAVE SEASONS?

In Europe, North America, and southern Australia, we have a cycle of changing seasons. Do you know what causes this cycle? The imaginary axis that runs through the earth (see p. 5) is tilted. As the earth travels around the sun once every year, the North Pole is tilted away from the sun for half a year and toward it for the other half. The same is true for the South Pole.

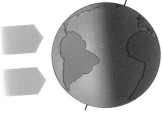

So different places in the world have more or less sunlight at different times of the year. When there are more hours of daytime than nighttime, it is summer. When there are more hours of nighttime than daytime, it is winter.

Understanding the seasons

The tennis ball represents earth and the knitting needle represents its imaginary axis. Ask an adult to help you stick the needle through the tennis ball. Now tilt the needle at an angle (about 23°) and stick one end into the styrofoam base.

Ask an adult to set up a lamp, with a low-wattage light bulb, in a dark place. This represents the sun.

Place your model earth, with its axis tilted toward the sun. This shows the position of the earth during midsummer in Europe and North America. (Remember that the earth rotates all the way around on its own axis once every 24 hours.) It is always daytime around the North Pole, and there is no sunlight around the South Pole. In southern Australia, the season is midwinter.

YOU NEED:

- an old tennis ball
- a knitting needle
- a block of styrofoam
- an electric lamp

See what happens to the seasons if you tilt the axis away from the sun.

Hot summers and cooler winters

Here are two activities that will help you to understand why summers are hot, and why winters feel much cooler.

Put the painted tin lids out in the sunshine. Slant them on the wooden block so that one faces toward the sunshine and the other faces away from the sunshine. Both lids must receive the sun's rays directly. After 15 minutes, touch the lids. See which one feels warmer.

Place the football on the ground and shine the flashlight directly onto the ball to form a circular patch of light. Then shine the flashlight beam at an angle, so that it forms a much larger patch of light on the football.

YOU NEED:

- 2 tin lids painted a dull black color (use the lids from empty cocoa tins or similar)
- 1 wooden block
- a flashlight
- a football

What has happened?

The lid that faced toward the sunshine was warmer than the one that faced away from the sunshine. Those parts of the earth that face more directly toward the sun get hotter than the parts that face away.

When the flashlight shone directly onto the football, it formed a strong patch of light. The sun's rays are more intense when they shine down directly on the earth. This happens during the summer. When the flashlight beam was at an angle, it formed a larger but weaker patch of light. In winter, the sunlit days are shorter and the sun's rays shine down in a slanting manner on the earth, so the earth does not get as hot as it does in summer.

Did you know?

An imaginary line runs around the middle of the earth, halfway between the North Pole and the South Pole. This line is called the equator. The earth is always hottest near the equator, because 2 to 3 times more sunlight falls on the equator than on the Poles.

SATELLITES AND UFOS

Do you know what stops the moon from falling down onto the earth? According to an old joke, the answer is moonbeams!

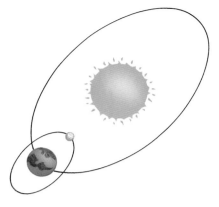

Surely this can't be true. If there were no force of gravity, the moon would speed away into space along a straight path. The pull of the earth's gravity prevents the moon from escaping in this way. Together, the force of gravity and the moon's tendency to move away act to make the moon orbit the earth along a path that is almost circular.

In a similar way, the sun's gravity stops the earth from shooting off into space and helps to keep the earth in its orbit around the sun.

YOU NEED:

- a small rubber ball
- sticky tape
- 1 metre of string
- an apple, with its core removed
- a thread spool

Putting a model moon in orbit

Tie one end of the string around the ball. Secure the string with the tape. Thread the other end of the string through the thread spool and then through the center of the apple. Tie the end of the string around the apple.

Take your model outdoors where the ball will not hit anything. Hold the spool and whirl the ball around in a horizontal circle above your head.

At first, the apple will be pulled up. Then you can keep the ball whirling in orbit around the spool.

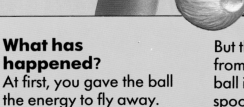

What has happened?
At first, you gave the ball the energy to fly away.

But the pull of gravity from the apple kept the ball in orbit around the spool.

Did you know?

Objects like the moon, which orbit the earth and other planets, are called satellites. Artificial satellites are built by engineers and sent up by powerful rockets to orbit the earth. Artificial satellites are used to transmit television and radio signals, to photograph the earth from up in space, and to help weather forecasters.

Strangers in the sky

Unidentified flying objects (UFOs for short) may appear in the sky. But if you know what to expect, these UFOs need not always puzzle you. Here are some strange sights to look for in the sky:

- balloons
- shooting stars
- moving lights (satellites, perhaps)
- the bright planet Venus
- flocks of birds
- saucer-shaped clouds.

Some people believe in the existence of "flying saucers" — spaceships that bring creatures from other planets. Other people have taken photographs of objects which they themselves have thrown into the air. They then claim that these are really alien spaceships.

You could prove how easy it is to trick some people by faking some UFO pictures yourself!

MEASURING FAR-AWAY OBJECTS

If you walk at a steady 4 miles per hour and take 1 hour to walk along the path to a village and back to where you started, how far away is the village?

You have walked 4 miles in 1 hour, but in this time you walked to the village and back again. So the village is half of this distance away, or 2 miles.

You cannot walk to the moon, but astronomers (scientists who study space) can measure the time it takes for a radar signal to be sent to the moon and bounced back to Earth. By halving the distance that the signal travels in this time, they can work out the distance to the moon. The average distance from the earth to the moon is 238,857 miles.

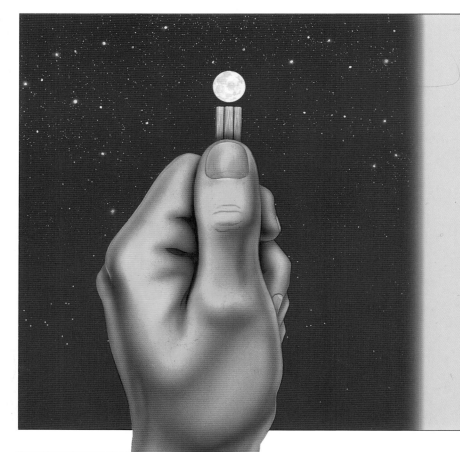

YOU NEED:

- several used matchsticks
- a metric ruler
- a tape measure
- a sheet of paper
- a pencil
- a pocket calculator

Measuring the moon

Here is a way that you can roughly measure the width of the moon.

Wait until the moon is a full one. Hold up several of the used matchsticks at arm's length, in front of the moon. Find how many matchsticks it takes to fit across the moon's diameter. (It will probably take three matchsticks.)

Did you know?

The sun and its family of nine planets is called the solar system. Look out for the planet Venus in the east at sunrise or in the west at sunset. It looks like a very bright star.

Radar is used to calculate the distance from Earth to the planets in the solar system. Other methods, based on geometry, have to be used to find the distance from the earth to the sun (about 94.6 million miles) and the nearer stars.

Now measure the total width of the matchsticks, in millimeters. Ask a friend to help you measure the distance between your eyes and the held-up matchsticks, also in millimeters.
Write down your answers:

Now do the following calculations on your pocket calculator:
Divide 384,400 by the distance from your eyes. Multiply the answer by the width of the matchsticks. The answer will give you roughly the diameter of the moon, in kilometers.

If the width of the matchsticks is 7 mm, and their distance from the eyes is 680 mm, the calculation is as follows:
384,400 ÷ 680 = 565
565 × 7 = 3,955
Answer: the approximate diameter of the moon is 3,955 kilometers (2,452 miles).

The true diameter of the moon is 3,476 kilometers (2,160 miles). How close to this is your answer?

AVERAGE DISTANCE TO THE MOON = 384,400 KILOMETERS (238,587 MILES)

DIAMETER OF THE MOON = ? KILOMETERS

WIDTH OF THE MATCHSTICKS = ...MILLIMETERS

DISTANCE FROM YOUR EYES = ...MILLIMETERS

13

WATCHING CLOUDS

When water is heated, some of it changes into a gas called water vapor. The water vapor rises up into the air where it cools and condenses, changing into tiny droplets of water. These droplets are as fine as dust. They float in the air as mist and cloud, and they may carry dirt and form dense fog.

Make your own clouds

Here are four different ways to make clouds.

Ask an adult to help you boil the water.

Watch the kettle as it boils. The water vapor itself is invisible, but it soon condenses in the cool air to form millions of water droplets, which you see as a white cloud.

Breathe out on a freezing cold day. The water vapor from your breath will condense as a smoky-looking cloud.

YOU NEED:

- a cold glass bottle
- warm water
- an ice cube
- a kettle of boiling water

Put some warm water in the bottle, which should be cold. Place the ice cube across the bottle opening. A cloud forms as water vapor from the air in the bottle is cooled by the ice.

Clouds in the sky

Clouds form in the sky when warm air that contains water vapor rises. Above the ground, the air pressure is less. The rising warm air expands and becomes cooler. This cooling makes the water vapor condense into droplets of mist or cloud.

Water vapor from the air close to the cold ground condenses to form mist. Mist is a cloud on the ground. Winds may force air carrying water vapor to rise over hills and mountains. Higher up, the air is cooler and so the water vapor condenses and changes into clouds.

Warm moist air rises

Blow hard into the cold bottle. When you stop blowing, a misty cloud forms on the inside of the bottle. Why?

What has happened?

You formed little clouds by making water vapor condense. When you stopped blowing into the bottle, you let the air inside the bottle expand, or take up more space. The pressure in the bottle became less. Lowering pressure on a gas is another way to make it cooler. So the water vapor from your breath condensed to form a mist.

Did you know?

There are four main types of cloud: cumulus clouds, cirrus clouds, stratus clouds and nimbus clouds. Here are some ways to identify the four types:

Light, fluffy cumulus clouds usually mean fine weather.

Wispy cirrus clouds often mean a change in the weather.

Gray stratus clouds could mean rain soon.

Dark stratus clouds are nimbus clouds, which bring rain or snow.

WHERE DOES RAIN COME FROM?

The air contains many tiny, almost invisible bits of dirt and salt, called dust particles. These particles help the water vapor in the air to condense, by giving the water something to stick to when the droplets form.

The dust-size droplets of water that float in the clouds move about in all directions. They bump into each other, stick together, and grow bigger. When they get too heavy to float, they fall as rain.

Remember the last way of making a cloud on p. 14? Before you repeat this experiment, ask an adult to light a match. Blow it out and hold the smoking matchstick inside the bottle. You should get a much better cloud this time.

Always ask an adult to help you when lighting matches.

Recording a week's rainfall

During rainy times of the year, the amount of rainfall varies from day to day.

YOU NEED:

- 7 narrow, flat-bottomed glass or plastic containers, with stoppers or caps (use empty spice jars, or old glitter tubes)
- a plastic soda bottle
- scissors
- 7 adhesive-backed labels
- a pencil

First, make a rainfall collector from the soda bottle. Cut the top off the bottle and turn it upside down to make a funnel. Cut the bottom off the bottle, about 5½ inches up from the base. Fit the funnel into this bottom section of the bottle.

Place your rain collector outside, in an open place where it will not be knocked over. You could wedge it between two rocks.

Do people remember the weather?

One day in the following week after you made your rainfall record, ask other people, both children and adults, if they can remember the driest and the wettest days from the previous week.

With your rainfall samples as proof, you can show them how reliable their memory has been!

Did you know?

If all the water vapor present in the atmosphere became liquid water, it could form a layer 1 inch deep all over the earth.

At the same time each day, for 7 days, empty any rain collected into one of the narrow containers. Label the container with the date and day of the week. Don't forget to label an empty tube on a dry day. Put the lid or stopper back on the container. At the end of the week you will have a display of your rainfall record for a whole week.

SNOW

Fierce, upward-blowing winds in thunderclouds hurl raindrops several miles up into the sky. Here it is so bitterly cold that the raindrops freeze into solid hailstones of ice.

Snow is formed more gently. In a yellowish-gray sky, at a temperature below freezing, water vapor starts to freeze, without first forming water droplets. The water vapor freezes to form delicate six-sided crystals of snow, or snowflakes. These crystals are shaped in beautiful ice patterns, and no two crystals are exactly alike.

Looking at snowflake patterns

Place the black cloth in a freezer until it is snowing outside. Then remove it from the freezer. Tie the handkerchief over your nose and mouth. This will stop your warm breath from melting the snowflakes.

Take the black cloth outside in the snow and let a few snowflakes fall onto it. Examine their patterns with your magnifying glass.

YOU NEED:

- a handkerchief
- a piece of black cloth
- a magnifying glass

Do this outdoors in a sheltered spot.

Did you know?

An American nicknamed "Snowflake" Bentley took photographs of thousands of snowflake crystals. He had them printed in a famous snowflake atlas. Try to draw a collection of snowflakes, similar to the ones you saw on the cloth.

YOU NEED:

- a glass jar
- a thermometer
- a yardstick
- warm clothing
- snow

Finding out about snow

See how much water you get when a jar full of snow melts.

When you build a snowman, time how long it takes for the snowman to disappear. Notice that it has to melt first before the snowman disappears.

Using the thermometer, see if the temperature on the surface of the snow is higher or lower than the temperature of the ground beneath the snow.

Notice in what ways the wind affects the snow.

Use the yardstick to measure whether the snow is the same depth everywhere.

Did you know?

The Inuits, who live in northern Canada, know how to cut hard-packed snow into blocks. They used to use the blocks to build their dome-shaped shelters, called igloos. A glassy piece of ice was used as a window, to let in the light. A tunnel, built from snow blocks, led to the igloo's door.

During snowy weather, see if you can build an igloo with your friends.

THUNDER AND LIGHTNING

All materials have two kinds of electric charge — a positive charge (written as +) and a negative charge (written as −). Normally, a material has equal amounts of positive and negative charges. But when materials rub together, the electric charges become separated. When these charges remain separated, they are given the name static electricity.

A material that loses negative charges is left with too many positive ones. It is said to be charged positively. A material that is left with too many negative charges is charged negatively.

YOU NEED:

- a woolen sweater

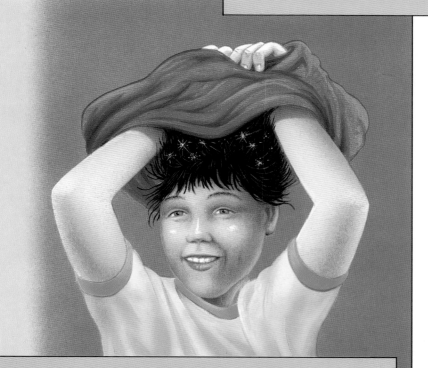

Electric sparks

Put on the woolen sweater on a dark night. In a dry room, pull off the sweater and notice what happens. You will feel the prickling of tiny electric sparks and see pale flashes of electricity. These tiny sparks are a miniature form of lightning.

What has happened?

When you pulled the sweater over your head, the wool rubbed against your hair. The wool became positively charged and your hair became negatively charged. The positive and negative charges pulled toward each other. They were attracted to each other. This attraction may have made your hair stand up.

The flashing sparks were caused by the negative charges from your hair being attracted to the wool's positive charges, and then jumping across.

Inside a thundercloud

When you watch dark thunderclouds rising rapidly through the sky, you can almost sense the huge amounts of energy inside them. Water droplets, ice crystals, and other particles swirl about inside the cloud, rubbing together. As a result, the top of the thundercloud may become positively charged, and the bottom part negatively charged with only some positive zones.

Charges of the same kind (negative and negative, or positive and positive) are called like charges. They push each other away, or repel each other. Charges of a different kind (negative and positive) attract each other. The negative charges at the bottom of the thundercloud are powerful enough to repel negative charges from the ground beneath. The ground then has too many positive charges and becomes positively charged.

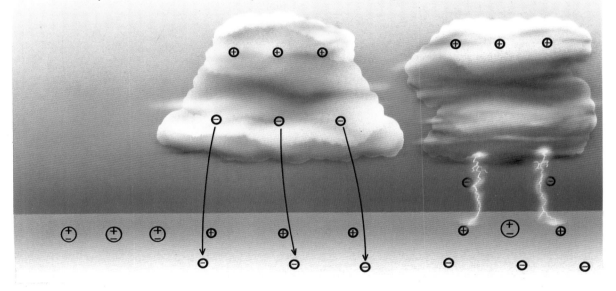

Lightning and thunder

During a storm, suddenly the negative charges in the thundercloud jump down. They are attracted by the positive charges on the ground. This happens as a zig-zag flash of lightning. The air becomes hot and glows in a brilliant flash. Thunder is caused by the heated air expanding and producing the loud sound of a thunderclap.

Did you know?

You can tell how far away a thunderstorm is by counting the seconds after you see a flash of lightning. Stop counting when you hear the thunder. Divide the number of seconds by 5, and the answer will be the distance in miles.

THE FORCE OF THE WIND

Wind is moving air. It is a powerful but invisible force. You can go out "wind watching" on a very windy day and make a list of all the things that are affected by the force of the wind, such as what happens to the birds on a windy day.

There are two main causes of wind. One is changes in air pressure. The other is the rotation of the earth on its imaginary axis. As the earth rotates, different parts of the earth are heated unevenly by the sun's rays, causing changes in air pressure.

A wind in your hand

YOU NEED:

- a sharp pencil
- paper
- scissors

Trace the propeller shape onto the paper and cut it out. Bend it along the dotted line across the middle. Balance your propeller on the pencil point.

Hold the pencil steady and away from any drafts. Warm air, heated by your hand, should make a rising wind to turn your propeller. You can also test your propeller over a warm radiator or a table lamp.

What has happened?

Many people know that "hot air rises," but perhaps they cannot explain why. Air takes up more space when it is heated. It expands, and so a certain amount of heated air has less mass, or air, in it than cold air. Mass gives air its weight, so hot air is lighter than cold air because it has less mass.

Gravity pulls more on cold air than on hot air, so cold air can push down with more pressure. The greater pressure of the cold air pushes up the hot air, making it rise. At the same time, a wind of cold air flows along the ground to take the place of the risen hot air.

Warmed air rose as a small wind to turn your paper propeller.

Recording wind direction

Bend the cardboard in half and staple it to one end of the straw. Push the screw into the other end. Balance the straw across your finger.

Push the pin through the straw's balancing point and into the eraser on the pencil end. Move the screw slightly until the straw balances on a level. This is your weather vane.

YOU NEED:

- a piece of cardboard 5 inches × 5 inches
- a stapler
- a metal screw
- a drinking straw
- a pencil with an eraser at one end
- a compass
- a sheet of paper
- a ruler
- a pin

Copy the octagonal, or eight-sided, "rose" onto the paper. Every day, at the same time, go out with your weather vane and compass. Hold the pencil steadily in your hand. The shorter end of the straw will point to the wind direction. Use your compass to find out the direction.

Draw a rectangle against the correct direction on your wind "rose." Write the date on it. Try to figure out the main, or prevailing, wind direction where you live.

Did you know?

You can get a good idea of the speed of the wind by looking at a copy of the Beaufort Wind Scale in an encyclopedia or weather book. The scale, which runs from 0 for calm weather to 12 for hurricane-force winds, describes the effects of wind as shown by smoke, trees, water, and buildings.

SOLAR HEATING

Energy from the sun is called solar energy. Rays from the sun take a few minutes to travel almost 95 million miles down to earth. This radiation from the sun lights up and heats the earth.

The plants and tiny animals that lived on earth millions of years ago obtained their energy from the sun. Today, the remains of those plants and creatures are believed to be the source of the fossil fuels — coal, gas, and oil — that we burn to give us other forms of energy, such as electricity.

Solar energy acts on the air around the earth to make winds, and on the water on land and in the air to make clouds and rain. So solar energy makes our weather.

Measuring solar heat

Even indoor heating is solar heating.

Copy the temperature chart shown below onto your sheet of paper. Ask an adult to help you to read the thermometer. Then take and record the temperature in the four places listed on the chart at 9 am, and at 12 noon. A thermometer measures heat in degrees Fahrenheit.

YOU NEED:

- a household thermometer
- a sheet of paper
- a pencil
- a ruler

		SUN	MON	TUE	WED	THU	FRI	SAT
Indoors	9:00 a.m.							
	12:00 p.m.							
Near the front door	9:00 a.m.							
	12:00 p.m.							
Out in the open	9:00 a.m.							
	12:00 p.m.							
Under a shady tree	9:00 a.m.							
	12:00 p.m.							

Where did the temperature change the most?

Where did the temperature change the least? Notice whether solar heating is most effective by day or by night.

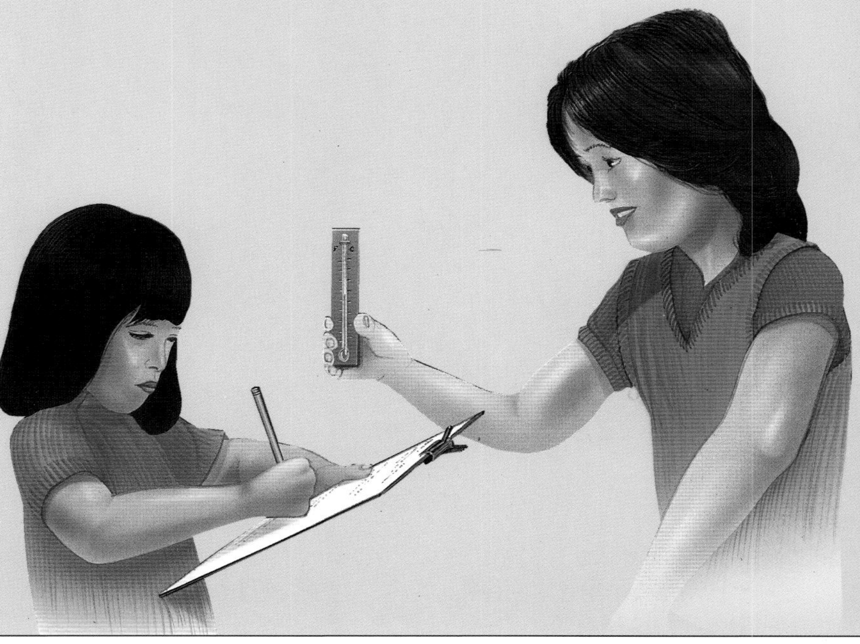

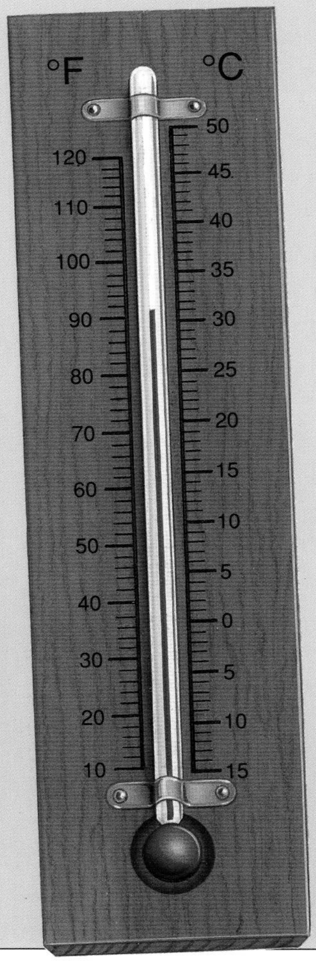

Fun in the sun

Fill the bottle with water to a depth of 1 inch. Add a few drops of food coloring or ink to the water. Mold the modeling clay around one end of the straw and push the other end into the water in the bottle. Use the clay to make a seal around the top of the bottle.

When you warm the bottle out in the sunshine or between your hands, some of the colored water rises inside the straw.

YOU NEED:

- water
- ink or food coloring
- a small, clear glass bottle
- a transparent drinking straw or narrow plastic tube
- softened modeling clay

What has happened?

The warmth from your hands, or from the sun's rays, warmed the air inside the bottle. The heated air got bigger, or expanded, and pushed the water up the straw.

YOU NEED:

- a pair of socks
- water
- a hot sunny day

Using solar energy to keep cool

Wet one of the socks and then wring out the water so the sock feels damp. Wear a sock on each foot while you lie out in the sunshine. The foot inside the damp sock will feel quite cold.

What has happened?

Solar energy heated the water in the damp sock and made it evaporate, or turn into a gas. As the water evaporated, it took away heat from your foot, keeping it cool.

Did you know?

In hot sunshine, evaporating sweat makes your skin feel cooler because it is taking heat away from your skin. Water from the sweat passes into the air next to your skin as water vapor. If a wind blows away this damp air, you lose more heat and feel colder. This effect is the wind chill factor.

EXTRA PROJECTS

YOU NEED:

- a straight stick
- a watch

Finding north with a shadow

Fix the stick upright in a flat piece of ground. Look at the stick's position at midday in winter (and at 1 o'clock in the summer). The shadow points toward the north.

In the Northern Hemisphere, the sun is in the south at midday so the sun casts the shadow of the stick toward the north. In the Southern Hemisphere, the sun is in the north at midday, and the stick's shadow points toward the south.

Some proverbs about the weather

Over hundreds of years, people have connected changes in the weather with different signs in nature. These ideas have led to sayings, or proverbs, which people tell when they want to forecast the weather.

Make your own observations to check if any of these proverbs are true.

- It is going to rain if ducks quack louder and more often.

- A ring around the moon means rain.
- It is going to be fine if the moon looks bright and clear.
- It is going to be windy if there is a yellow sunset.
- It is going to be a frosty morning if the sunset is salmon colored.

YOU NEED:

- a water mister or hosepipe

A rainbow in your garden

Do not try this activity if there is a garden hose ban in your area.

Go out into the backyard in the early morning or late afternoon, when the sun is shining low down in the sky. Stand with your back to the sun and spray water away from you. If you look carefully into the mist of drops, you will see a circular rainbow.

What has happened?

The drops of water acted like tiny prisms. The drops split the sunlight into the colors of the rainbow and then reflected the colors back into your eyes.

A rainbow may look circular when it is seen from an airplane.

An observatory for clouds

Place the mirror on flat ground outdoors. Be careful not to point the mirror up at the sun. Put the compass in the middle of the mirror. Turn the compass so that its pointer is over the N, or north point, on the dial. Move the mirror so that the pointer is pointing to one of the mirror's sides.

Observe the reflections of the clouds in the mirror.

- Notice in which direction they are moving.
- Are they cumulus, cirrus, stratus, or nimbus clouds?
- Can you see two layers of cloud traveling in different directions?

A book on weather from your local library will help you to identify clouds more accurately. See if you can learn how to use clouds to forecast the weather.

YOU NEED:

- a mirror
- a compass

GLOSSARY

A

artificial
Describes anything that is not natural but is made by people

attract
To pull toward

axis
An imaginary rod that passes through the North and South poles. The earth turns around this axis once every 24 hours

B

Beaufort Scale
A scale of wind speeds, from 0 (calm) to 12 (hurricane)

C

condensation
The change from a gas to a liquid, when the gas cools

crystal
A solid form of a substance, in which the atoms are arranged in an orderly way

D

diameter
The widest part of a circle

E

eclipse
When an object goes into the shadow of another object in space, or is hidden from sight by another object getting in the way.

electric charge
A particle of electric substance. There are two types of electric charge — positive and negative.

electricity
Energy that is connected with moving, or static, electric charges

Equator
An imaginary line that passes around the middle of the earth, halfway between the North and South poles

evaporate
When a liquid is heated and turns into a gas

F

fossil fuel
A fuel substance, such as coal, oil, and gas. Fossil fuels formed in the ground from the remains of plants and animals that lived on earth millions of years ago.

G

gravity
A force that pulls objects downward by attracting them

H

hail
Lumps of ice that form when water droplets freeze inside thunderclouds

hemisphere
Half of a sphere, such as the earth's Northern and Southern hemispheres

L

lightning
A huge electric spark produced when electric charges jump from a cloud to the earth, or from the earth to a cloud

M

mass
The amount of material in a substance

O

octagonal
Having eight sides

orbit
The path in space of a satellite, traveling around a planet, or of a planet traveling around a star

P

pressure
The amount of force pushing on a certain area

prevailing
The chief or main force, such as a prevailing wind

prism
A triangular piece of transparent glass or plastic that splits light into the colors seen in rainbows

R

repel
To push away

rotate
To turn around an axis

S

satellite
A moon that orbits a planet; also, an artificial object sent up to orbit a planet or a moon

solar
Anything to do with the sun

solar system
The sun, together with its planets and their satellites

star
A huge ball of extremely hot gases in space. The sun is a star

T

temperature
A measurement of how hot or cold a substance is

thermometer
An instrument for measuring temperature

V

vapor
A gas

W

weight
The force of gravity pulling on a mass gives it weight

INDEX